The Fourth Quarter

David Craig:
Cheltenham,
april 10 2008

For Anne, beloved fellow poet

'Confederacy of shadows, intertwined destinies and death, people and all they leave behind, in a drawer, in a closet, on an empty canvas or a blank page. And despite everything we fight to hold onto the heat of the object, the force of the brushstroke, the footprint of the man who walks…'

(Carlos Fuentes, *This I Believe*)

The Fourth Quarter

David Craig

Published 2005
by

STACK
BOOKS

Smokestack Books
PO Box 408, Middlesbrough TS5 6WA
Tel : 01642 813997
e-mail : info@smokestack-books.co.uk
www.smokestack-books.co.uk

Cover design and print by
James Cianciaruso
j.cianciaruso@ntlworld.com

Cover: Illustration by Ulrike Kanne
Photograph of David Craig
by Andy Rafferty

ISBN 0-9548691-7-6

Smokestack Books
gratefully acknowledges the support of
Middlesbrough Borough Council
and Arts Council North East.

Smokestack Books is a member of
Independent Northern Publishers
www.northernpublishers.co.uk

Contents

First Strawberries

It is in me always,
That tang of green leaves bruised from heaping fruit
Whose scarlet cheeks sweat with the summer's dew
Onto the scrubbed brown draining-board,
The chill white Belfast sink,
The fish-grey floor.
That August's crop, it is always here
Year after year. How many are in store ?
Perhaps there will be twenty more.

One of Theirs

When I was flying a Spitfire during the War
In that momentous summer of '41,
I used to launch it from the top of a stook
In a hayfield bleaching under the sun.

It was powered by a skein of twisting elastic
And however tightly I tensioned it,
My plane careered briefly above the stubble
And plummeted like a Messerschmitt.

One day we saw a single Heinkel,
Black cross on the blue above Kildrummy farm,
And heard its chug - only a lone marauder -
No serious cause for alarm.

Next week, when dancers left the Hall for a breather
And a drag on a Woodbine or a Craven A,
Another marauder saw the glow beneath him
And sent his bombs away.

All they trashed was a field of turnips
But still, the smokers should have had more sense.
Did they not realise that my balsa Spitfire
Was their only defence ?

Sand Shot

My father's head appears at the lip of the bunker :
'Why can't you stand away ?'
Sandstorms followed, flurry after flurry.
Voice from the depth, 'I will he here all day !'

Speyside encompassed us, a sultry garden,
Birches wafting their lace, the bronze-limbed pines.
If only my ageing father
Could score some 4s instead of 7s and 9s...

At last the ball shoots out, it clears the green
And vanishes quick and white as a rabbit's scut.
My father throws his niblick almost at me
As I prepare to putt.

No more fun that morning.
A sticky end to uncomplicated joy.
Amongst the blues of sweltering summer mountains
I was no longer a boy.

An Incident at Ely

The railway line from Aberdeen to Cambridge
Spans like a girder. Mohawk steel-erectors
Who stroll six hundred feet above Manhattan
Without a safety-line might be less easy
On this low wire, this bridge between two cultures.

My girlfriend's father has died. I track back north
In a January blizzard. The engine pauses,
Breathing heavily, as we face the Forth.
A cantilever climbs the sky and vanishes
Into the locust flakes, steep as the Pinnacles
Of Liathach disappearing into cloud.

The humorous man is lost to us. Terrified
By prostate cancer, he has dropped himself
Into the North Sea south of Girdle Ness
Down a deep geo where grey-green water lurches,
Bashing on rock-walls clarted with guano.

In arctic water, changing your mind too late,
Do you thrash frantically back to shore
Before your mind goes blank ?
                              The blizzard eases,
The locomotive shrieks, the river glints
Down there amongst the swarming flakes.
                              Three days
Go by, the body has been identified,
Surrendered, cremated. I wish that I could cry.

The train back south pulls slowly through a cutting
Cleft in the granite just above that geo.

This time it's fog that veils the wintry waters
And fog the whole way south. I sit in a box
Of shuddering glass and plywood, watching steam
Blear into mist above the frozen fields
Of turnips, cabbages and winter wheat.

East Anglia might be Russia. We must change
At Ely where the cathedral rears its bulk
Like some earthbound Titanic. Stupor of cold
And numbness of fatigue and disbelief
Are hunching me deep into my coat. Inside
The Ladies Waiting Room a heap of coals
Gives out small heat from a cast-iron grate
And everyone gathers there, not talking, sitting
Tethered to scanty luggage. Just on midnight
Two men come in, in bluish showerproof coats,
Their eyes as grey as pencil-lead, their cheeks
Shaven like polished bone. 'Get out,' they say
To the men among us. 'This is the Ladies Room.'

'The other room was locked,' we feebly protest,
And 'This is the only fire' and 'There's no harm…'

'Improper use of this facility
Is an offence.' The plainclothes men's expressions
Have altered less than a stone crossed by a shadow,
A wave in which a man has drowned. We go
And stand in the fuming twilight, stamping our feet
Like unemployed men during the War, in winter,
Scraping at scabs of snow with iron shovels.

Why were we so submissive ? I can blame
The funeral aftermath, the midnight hour,
The fog and cold that clamped the continent
From Peterborough to Poland to the Urals…
How could we let ourselves be herded so ?
There were no whips or guns or cattletrucks,
Only the spineless habit of obedience
Which makes us meek at our own humiliations
And silent about the murdering of others.

The Oldest Member

When the destroying flames seethed through the clubhouse
Roaring like traffic, crackling like rifle-shots,
Most of the lockers were consumed - the mashies
And niblicks burned from the handle to the head,
Leaving their metal blades in red-hot heaps
Like furnace slag. The drivers, spoons and brassies
Were turned to charcoal. Only the newest clubs
With their metal shafts survived - my father saw them
Laid out in rows on the grass outside the ruin
'Twisted like pipe-cleaners'.
                    Mr Lorimer
Had never been able to afford a locker
And so his bag of hickory-shafted clubs
Was still on his shoulder fifty-six years later
When he died on the 17th hole. He had sliced as usual,
Into the whins as usual. He left the others
(The Reverends Gray and Milne and Dr Gorrie)
And disappeared into the prickles, making his sound
That could be spelt as 'Tissa-tissa'. His ball
(Pink to be visible in the snow) was lying
In a glade where yellowhammers nested in June
And whin-flowers breathed their essence of peach and almond
Into the salty breezes.
                    Mr Lorimer
Was lying beside it, his favourite mashie-niblick
Clutched in his fingers, which were knobbed and rosy
As though with permanent chilblains. His yellowed dentures
Were bared in a kind of grin and his open eyes
Of faded North Sea green were fixed on the sky
As though, in December, he could still make out
Poised at the zenith the quick black pulse of a skylark.

The Great Ice Animal

It was nothing much, the glacier,
My first, the Fox, South Island.
It was the forehead of an elephant,
Wrinkled and scarred, exhausted, venerable,
Staggering as his own great weight
Forced his own legs into the ground.

He had been strong enough in his prime
To score black horizontals
Along the bounding rockwalls
And dump a trillion tons
Of livid gravel onto the floor
His ponderous bulk had bulldozed.

Rain-squalls drench the tired grey beast.
His hide splits into fissures
Baring his sea-green bones.
A hundred camera flashes struggle
To catch his godlike features
At this juncture of their dying.

In 1955 - the notice said,
A full mile down the roadway -
The ice-front had been here,
Here where the ngaio and puriri trees
Lift up their blossomy heads
And living water jumps from the rocks.

Mount Cook puts forth its strength,
A white brain in the cloudy maelstrom -
Its withered extremities barely answer,
Its spinal cords are numb.
The blank authority of the warming globe
Has civilised the barbarous ice.

Blind Man's Weather

'Hold out your hands,' she said, and so he laid them
On the worktop by the window facing the garden,
The palms cupped upwards, trusting.
When the cold weight settled into them,
He did not flinch. 'Oh let me guess,' he said,
Feeling her breast breathing against his back.
'It's ice,' he said, 'an icicle' - he stroked
The dewy sleek of it.

                    'Near enough,' she said,
'It's -'

    'Let me guess !' He laid it on the formica
And spanned it with his fingers, running their tips
Along the sheer and hard of it, then setting
His hands against its ends. '12 centimetres.
Or 13. And it's solid. And it's strong.'
He had thought, a brittle flute. This was a core,
A pillar from a house of ice, a piston
From winter's humming engine. 'From the pipe -
The outfall's frozen solid ?' - settling his head
More snugly backwards in the cleft of her.
Her silent laughter trembled into his bones,
He concentrated. He held and hefted it
Between bunched finger ends, he stood it up,
Guarding against a fall, then smoothed his cheek
Against the wintry numb of it, let it roll
Its moist along his forehead, brought the hairs
Of his nostrils to its frost. It was odourless
As space, sheer as the jet-stream. All it had culled
From Earth's rank juice and tangle was its own
Essence of pureness, shine of the sky made liquid,
Weight of the raindrops moulded, clouds distilled…
'You took it from my gauge,' he said, uncertain
Whether to laugh or quarrel.

                                   'Well - you left it
To crack or thaw in the garden when we went
To Devon on the Sunday.'
                              'Seven days -
'I am holding seven days !' He wanted them
Solid between his hands, wanted their life
Never to melt or drain. It could not be.
He took the core in one hand, hers in the other,
Stepped with her onto the grass, and hurled those days
With all his strength far upwards unto the sun.

Solitary Music

The bleached strings of the grass are playing -
Bending low I barely catch the chord
That hisses over the steely frets
Of the winter-hammered sward,

A music entire and single,
As sparing of melody or trill
As a Saharan singer bowing his one-string bass
Beside an empty well,

He is in his torrid, I in my freezing country,
Nothing in common linking man to man
Except the notes of that solitary music
Vibrating down the meridian.

You are Me

This is not me, this curdled flesh
Like dough that will not rise.
In the cruel cross-light, under my mirrored eyes,
The imperfections shine.

Stomach that was so tense and Tarzan-like
When I first made love -
Now I can see it easily from above,
That hairy bulge, which I can still draw in,
When I remember to. But then,
Most of the time my memory
Is faulty as a cut-price ansafone.

No wonder, since it lives
Inches beneath that nearly naked skull
('Not baldness,' says the dirty post-card, 'but
A solar panel for a sex-machine'
Or any other fantasy
Cooked up by hacks to tickle ageing men).

I little thought to see
Between my Adam's apple and my chin
A looseness like the wattle of a cockerel
Or a woman's earlobe pendulous with gold
In the markets of Ceylon.

Oh wintry stubble, oh grave marks on the hand
Like blotches on a gull's egg - you are me,
And while I acknowledge you as mine
I'll take my glasses off again and see
Those images grown softer
Under the atomising grains of time,
Under its water.

Melanoma

Now he is out in the open I can see him
Waving his pincers at me. Cancer the Crab.
Nothing to do with spellbound constellations -
This is the luck of flesh.
Some crumb of my red marrow flinched as it formed,
Quailed as the weakness sealed itself in,
Began to bide its time.

The miniature time-bomb ticked,
Decades not minutes trickled through the glass.
As the Sahara masses outwards,
The Dead Sea dies some more,
The dark-brown marks on my back
Wake from their lifetime's sleep
And busy themselves. 'How now, old mole,
Dost work in the flesh so fast ?'

The surgeon's cuts are shallow - good prognosis.
Now they will see me regularly
Four times a year until…
'If need be we will chop away some more.'

My moves along the rock-face, over the drop,
Have usually been irreversible.
The rope is there, the protection gear
Moulded from adamant alloy, the company
Of another breathing body.
Now I am soloing. My limbs, mine alone,
Will see me right. Or not.
My mind, enthralled, spectates
As the slow-motion fall accelerates.

Growth

Since the surgeons told me they had found
A lump in my armpit, and instructed Sister
To 'move it up and down against the rib',
Things are defaulting on me. Gritstone houses
As dense and brown as loaves
Are turning transparent, I can almost see
The leafless trees behind them
As if through a pane of stone. My own fragility
Is seeping into the world. Look, look -
Everything phases itself out, melts, gives up…

Or in another mode : they turn away
From me, their windows close down blank as eyelids,
Cold-shouldering me as patently shoddy stuff -
They know full well that whether I survive
Another eleven months or eleven years,
They will outlast me. (They will anyway.)
Why make this poem if in another year
Or ten I will not be here ?
Why should my tune last longer than its echo ?
What have I thought I was crafting, pyramids
Or Easter Island faces ? Only one phrase
Of mine will still be legible
In the 27th century - those letters
On a greenslate gravestone planted in Bassenthwaite :
W.P. 'AT HOME IN THE STEEP PLACES'.

In a bad hour everything looks it.
A crumpled, airless football left in the lane
Is an operating theatre remnant
Bound for the incinerator.
A child's tent in a garden with its flap
Tied back is horribly vacant. (I was the boy
Who left it yesterday.)

When Hardy races past me, black paws scudding,
He is outdistancing me
For good ; and almost anyone under forty
With a smooth skin and all their hair
Is crazily unaware that they are stepping
Nimbly towards senility.

I cling to you like a drowning man,
  Pull you against my chest.
You let me snuggle into you,
  My hand around your breast.

You are the centre of my life
  (The life that I still have).
If only the two of us could step
  Together into the grave !

This is the selfishness of pain
  For if my love is deep,
I should agree to turn away
  As when we go to sleep.

The condition (cancer) and the person (myself)
Reeled towards each other over the years,
Capsules slowly converging. Now they have docked -
'Rape !' the Soviet spacemen used to cry
As the new arrival fitted in.
                    The surgeon
Is using homely words : 'We will take away
Everything except the nerves and muscles'
(That's sound, just what I would have done myself).
'The drains are rather a gamble, but presently
The lymph will find its own way through your body.'
A cool, managerial voice, the green eyes steady

Above his plump cheeks fledged with steely stubble.
Steady is good. I want him perfect, perfectly
Drawing his scalpel round below my armpit,
No tremor, no indecision, his focus fine
As a kestrel flickering over its prey, then still
As a cloud in Nevada, brain become all eye,
Sharpening and fining-down each grass-blade, wind-twitch,
Bee-shadow, mouse-breath, muscle-fibre, nerve-end,
Blood-vessel, vein-valve, lymph-gland, cancer-nodule…
The steel beak is sure. It feels and knows.
The hit is imminent. This programme cannot stop.
The invisible brain distils its brilliant drop.

There is a vile submissiveness in this
Acceptance of the surgery
(Shaving of armpit, sliding in of needle,
The cut from the front beneath the arm, and down) :
Too like a thief in Arabia who meekly
Lays his wrist on the block ;
Too like a condemned man in Arkansas
Who moves on his own feet towards the chair.
I have done no crime and yet
The whole thing bullies me like a punishment
And this is true
Not only of the illness but of the treatment.

If I am living on borrowed time,
    What is the interest rate ?
What happens to me if I fail to return it
    On the appointed date ?

In a good hour all colours flow back in.
The lords-and-ladies thrust their scrolls
Greener than ever out of the wayside earth.
The first, late coltsfoots of this shivering March

Shine upwards like inverted suns.
The climbing rose, renewed
By our own brand of ruthless surgery,
Throws shoots as red as sea-anemones
Along our eastern wall.
It is too early yet to say
Whether the coming season will be fine,
Therefore the bulletins of this poem
Must be provisional
But then, so are we all.

The Good Patient

As I pass through the automatic doors
Security welcomes me,
Dressed in white, laminated in white,
Deployed in sunlit rooms
Smelling of polish and chrysanthemums.

There is nothing wrong with me
That they can't fix, nothing that they don't know.
Of course it isn't true and yet
This lot are totally expert.
They know how soon my blood will clot,
Each stitched scar on my back,
How fast my heart will beat and miss and beat again,
Trudging and halting on its wayward track.

They map each corrugation of my bowel,
The flecks and fidgets of my albumen,
They trace the scarlet branching of the tree
Inside each shadowy lung,
Scanning through muscle for the essential me.

Foolish to call them saints -
There is nothing specially virtuous about these
Masters and mistresses of plumbing,
Embroidery and carpentry.
What we admire about them
Is simply their omnipotent expertise.

That trolley of pills is sure to see me right,
That drip will drip all night
And I can switch the pain off when I please.

How good to read and write
In this aseptic sanctuary,
As single-minded as a monk
Who has bartered freedom for security
And worships health (his own) and seeks salvation
In the bloody communion of the operation.

What I Am

As I slide off the operating table
I catch sight of a part of me
In the bottom of a silvery alloy cup.
A second later, Theatre Sister
Has clapped her hand across it like a lid.
She keeps it there.

It was the merest morsel,
A scarlet scrap of lean beef mince
With a dark-brown spot in the centre.
Yes, I consist of that -
Meat that a raptor might have fancied,
A cannibal eager to make his own
Whatever strength it contained.

Inside my skull is a greyish sponge,
Gelatinous, with a salty flavour -
Yes, I consist of that.
In the most vibrant part of it
A honeycomb of giant molecules
Creates the whole of my knowledge, memories, loves.

Four hundred thousand generations resulted
In this particular mix,
Steered it through death and chaos, let it be.
It works, it hangs together,
These seventy kilos of tissues soft and hard :
They are enough for me.

Shetland Refugee

Between the weltering brain-grey fracto-nimbus
And the salt maelstrom
A lone crane labours, cruciform wings
And lank legs dangling like an unbalanced mobile.

She is a hero of survival,
Precariously straddling the air-waves,
A trapeze artiste who's losing
Her routine between the swoop and the upswing.

Did the Picts ever see one
Navigating unsteadily above
Their long walls on the spine of the Ness,
A far cry from her goal in Sweden ?

Among these alien gannets and fulmars
She cannot browse on tranquil water-meadows.
Their jet and turquoise eyes
Bore through the spume, unseeing her.

Helplessly westering, she's lost her comrades.
As her fat burns up, the lizards
And seeds of Algeria leach from her system, wiping
The memory of those thrumming wings beside her.

She will not be carrion
So long as the eye of the cyclone spins on southward
And the Gulf Stream breathes again,
So long as the Arctic Circle can embrace her.

The midnight sun will ripen like a yolk
In the sky's white oval
And the whole flock skirl
From their coiling throats to greet the last arrival.

At the Western Rim

Ensay, Barra, Jura, Mingulay

Black island on the white gold of the sound,
Mote in the sea's vision,
Entice me to see you through the water
Running down my cheeks.
Lure me to comb your beaches
For the jetsam of your lives
And read the whorls of your palms and fingers.

Here the hachures of the lazybeds
Are ribs beneath the skin of the island.
As the families grew
They drove their hungry spades
To the very lip of the bluff.
When the potatoes were lifted
They nearly tumbled into the sea.

There the throat of the dale
Wears the links of the river
Like silver torcs. On the other side
Of the hill the grandsons of the cleared
Ploughed the reclaiming furrows
With a pair of horses in the traces,
A black and a white, their loose manes rippling.

Here the red deer lift their heads
From a drink of the river, drooling
Skeins of it from their lips
As they stare at the car's blue hull
In placid wonderment. Adders twine
Under recumbent stones and slowworms ease
Their pregnant bellies between the brackens.

There the houses are empty as eggshells,
Windows blinded by sandblow.
Catherine and Mary Maclean, Teresa and Annie MacNeill,
Black ringlets framing grown-up smiles,
Look out at us from under the thatch.
Their feet were bare in the hay
As they followed their parents' sickles
Between the Sea of Ghosts and the Port of the Dead.

The Rape and Old Age of Morag

She sees him out of the corner of her eye -
She turns to face him - he has hidden again
Behind the angle of the lambing-pen.
She sees him in silhouette against the sky
Where sandstone bulges like a dinosaur.
She sees him in the fox-head on the fence,
Rows of triangular quartz-white teeth that clench.
She sees him blocking the oblong of the door.
She sees him in the raven-hair that gleams
On the close-cut rounded head of her little son.
She sees him through the barrel of a gun
Eyeing her down its spiralling oily sheen.
She sees him in the midden, tapering red.
And in the stain above her single bed.

What had he said to her, the night he forced her,
Then slithered from the bedclothes, wiping his legs ?
'Breathe a word and they'll turn you out to beg.'
Next he had tried to win her round with banter,
Bringing his pink lips inches from her ear :
'Cheer up, Morag ! You mustn't look so sad !
Like me a little, girl - I'm not all bad.
Why should a bit of fun end up in tears ?'
Feeling his 'loving' touch she bit his hand,
Gagged on his taint of brandy and cigarettes,
Panicked for fear her blood had stained the sheets,
Started to feel her irreversible wound,
And still said nothing, making herself not cry
But if she had a baby, she would die.

They moved to a stony croft along the coast,
Father and Mother, Morag and little Don.
In early July, when the clipping work was done,
She went to the shore and put him to her breast,

Feeling his small lips tickle for the milk.
Out in the loch the ebb had bared the rocks.
The drying weed was ticking like a clock,
The idle water stretched as grey as silk
Towards America. She would take the boat,
Put milk in a bottle, cuddle Don in his shawl.
Maybe they'd drown in the whirl of the overfall
Where Cailleach Bheur rinsed through her sodden clout.
Maybe the three white Birds of Bride would come,
Swathe them in bog-cotton, carry them home.

The minister arrived in a blast of hail.
'Desperate, desperate for the time of year !
I had great trouble getting up from the shore.
How are you all ? And how is the little - ' Wail
Upon wail was greeting him from the corner crib.
The family stared at him, and on and on
The kettle stayed unboiled, the soda scone
Unmargarined. He lurched towards the babe,
His black coat flapping. Mother's voice came low :
'You can do nothing for us, bless or curse,'
And Morag carried Don upstairs to nurse,
Hating the man of God, who had tried to do
That thing which her own father had never done.
And never would - give comfort to her son.

Always he seemed to be sitting underwater,
Father in Grandpa's chair beside the range.
On thundery mornings when the light was strange
He would stare as though he had never seen his daughter.
Dark in the Black Watch tartan in his picture
Taken the month before he went to France,
He was the man who had never had a chance
To escape from a life he saw as pure affliction.

When Uncle poached a salmon, he refused
To touch it, saying, 'That was not meant for you'.
Two speeches she remembered, only two
From all the condemning, judging words he had used :
'Always remember, Morag, what you have done.'
'It would have been safer if we had had a son.'

When Don was three, she took him to the haven
Where red rock parted to let in the tide
To the very lip of the croft. On either side
Rose sharp towers looming like the Prow of Blaven
Across the Inner Sound. Beneath the glistening
Pane of a tidal pool a sunken garden
Of seaweeds blossomed. She felt her four years' burden
Slide from her back. She sang, and Don was listening,
'Row me across to the islands.' Limpet shells
Lay in the crevices - they gathered them,
Launched them like little boats and watched them skim
On choppy wavelets, grounding on the shoals
Of bladder-wrack, parting and sailing on.
When they looked up, the afternoon had gone.

Mother was watching when they went for eggs
To the rushes of the out-by ; when she washed
His dirty bottom ; watching as she brushed
His stiff black hair, or soothed his angry legs,
Lumpy from nettle-stings with leaves of docken ;
Watching them when she slapped his sticky fingers
Scarlet with stolen jam - till Morag's anger
Festered with questions that could not be spoken :
What are you watching, Mother ? What are you seeing,

The brute's face surfacing in the little boy's ?
A gentleman's temper in the bairnie's cries ?
She ached with words in the centre of her being
And still said nothing. Neither of them spoke.
All words had foundered when her waters broke.

She saw the Lodge as hell now, lurking under
The humped, star-blotting outline of the Bheinn.
It was a kind of pit for dirty men.
A place where beasts and criminals would go
To build their torture chambers. Over the years
Their cars got bigger, wilder music sounded
On August evenings. Then the place was blinded,
The windows shuttered. Brambles and rusting wires
Strangled the lords' and ladies' paradise.
They would be back, or foreigners would come
To fish and kill. It had never been a home,
The 'castle' in the forest, hidden from eyes
Of visitors and crofters, where the swine
Mounted each other, drowned in tubs of wine.

When Donald was gathering buckies on the shore
With Uncle's red-haired twins from Alta-na-Feidh,
She sat and listened, hiding in the lee
Of the Blaven-towers. She heard the redheads swear :
'Bugger off, Donny ! The biggest ones is mine.'
'You bugger off !' A howl of grief - a splash
Flat as the down-fall of a jumping fish.
She rose to her feet - heard little Angus whine,
'Leave me alone. And leave my brother be,
You filthy bastard.' Not a word from Don.
Then, 'I'm not crying. I'll never cry again.
None of you's big enough to frighten me.'
A little later, 'I'll fight you both.' And once,
'I'm crying because my Dad was killed in France.'

Mother was dying of tuberculosis.
Her voice came maundering from the upper room :
'Never ask for money ! When'll he come ?
Morag my darling, your cheeks are pink as roses…'
Where should she go, to the road at Tigh-na-Greine
Where neighbours were, the postie and the nurse ?
She could not face them. Allt-na-Feidh was worse -
Uncle was there - the mountain stood between -
The waters would boil a thousand feet below -
Don would delight in it - her head would reel
With the white swirling, like the path to school
On days of spate, eleven years ago…
She sat, and Mother cried out overhead,
Spilling her last blood on her marriage bed.

They settled into their days. Their long days turned
Like swathes beneath the scythe. The channel flowed
Into the loch and out again. Like roads
The tidal currents shimmered blue, or burned
To embers at the close of another year.
In sultry July the twins would come and clip -
Straightening their backs to watch a distant ship,
Cracking a sheep-tick on the collie's ear -
Then left 'to earn good wages' down the coast.
Don was immune to money, took his rod
And disappeared behind Bheinn Ruadh-side.
She rarely saw him watching for the post.
His world was all inside him, turned down low,
Listening to Irish on the radio.

Once when he went to Perth to buy a dog
He passed through Kyle, stood by the harbour wall
And watched the shingle under-water crawl
And teem with feeding crabs. He heard the drag

And clack of avid pincers, felt them close
On crumbs of flesh, saw the plate-armoured back
Of the one great crab-animal print its black
On a white carcase lying in the ooze.
It was like looking into a brain and seeing
The layered thoughts stir with a pulse of pain or fear.
Maybe his father's remains were lying here -
Maybe it was like that when he was dying
'Lost in the Gulf' soon after he had 'gone
To Texas' and would be 'sending for them soon.'

He was himself whenever he took his rod
Far up behind Bheinn Ruadh to a lochan
Dark as a starless night, its glaze unbroken
By any gull or otter. It lay hid
Below a buttress and a tottering stack.
Two trout would rise in a spellbound afternoon.
He would grow small and still as though he had been
Unborn again into the womb of rock.
He was himself when digging out a cairn.
Foxes had had the meat of forty lambs.
His terrier crawled back out, died in his arms
Matted in fox-blood, cradled like a bairn.
He was himself when Mother, clutching her head,
Told him his father raped her in her bed.

She sat in the home-made armchair, feeling her feet
Throb like two yeasty loaves about to rise.
She irked and hotched, trying to be at ease
Or Don would be furious, battering at the peats
With the old fire-tongs. He was on the hill,
Levelling this telescope along his legs.
The sheep on the distant path were close as bugs

Grandpa had spoken of, clustering down his kilt
In pleated lines. He had tried to see his own
Face in the Black Watch photograph, his nose
Pinched at the nostrils, the meeting of his brows…
All that they had in common was the frown.
What was he ? He was a person. He was one
Of a trillion blobs of life. He was a man.

Nobody dreamed that he would die before her.
She was familiar, white hair in the porch.
The men from Tigh-na-Greine, off to catch
The crabs and lobsters or line for plaice off Morar,
Would wave to her - could she see them ? Up on the slope
The tall, round-shouldered figure of her son
Would scythe the short hay, laying green on green,
Or stride with his dog and cromach after his sheep.
On the calm of a rainy day she still heard nothing
At eleven in the morning from his room.
She hirpled through to his bedroom in the gloom
And saw beneath the quilt no rise of breathing,
No crimp on his   sunburnt forehead, not a trace
Of feeling in his stony-sculptured face

Where over and over she had looked for anger,
Some quirk of humour, or a blench of pain.
All this could not have vanished from his brain !
She beat on his chest with fists, with failing fingers,
With sweating palms that badgered and caressed.
Nothing. She took a sheet from the press and hung
It up in the pinetree. Before the day was done
The fishermen came to her through the mist
And carried Don to the haven. Like a spectre
One heron left the rocks and flapped off low.

Nobody said a word. They watched it go
On shrouding wings above the sluggish water.
Her heart broke then. She had nothing left to give.
Why should she be the one condemned to live ?

She sees him close behind her, darkly reflected
In the window facing seaward, stooping outline
Superimposed on the washed turf of the shoreline,
Standing among the curlews, looking dejected.
She sees him in the hound's-tooth-check deerstalker
Hung on the hooks for Visitors. She sees him
In Father's photo. (What can she do to please him ?)
She sees him in the brown face of the doctor
Who called to give her 'something for her fever'
And listened to her heart. She sees his face
In the Sheltered Housing garden, in the space
She has made her own, while over and over and over
She counts the days they spent together alive :
Sixteen thousand two hundred and twenty-five.

Migrants

A crofter stands at her door in Ormacleit
And fixes her eyes on Rome.
Of course she cannot make out
The campanile or the dome
Of her favourite saint with the same name as her brother
Peter, named by her mother
After her own Peter drowned at sea
Twelve weeks into her pregnancy.

Her thoughts wing off like corncrakes
Heading for Egypt when the summer is past,
Brown birds most articulate at night
Who lurk in the roots of the pasture,
Secretive, rarely visible in the daylight.
She sees them crossing Biscay
And the stepping stones of the Balearic Islands
Two thousand miles from the Highlands

To make their landfall somewhere in Italy.
Now she is worried. How will her prayers
Survive the maelstrom of the sea ?
It eats at the fringe of the machair, makes her crawl
In the lee of the graveyard wall
When she has gone to read the granite stones
Marking the places where the Peters,
Her father and her brother, left their bones.

She looks back to her years of work in London,
In Lewisham's crowd and shops -
Another stage in the southerly migration
Which never falters, never stops -
A loop in a driven programme.
Does she not know that few get through ?
Will she ever face that blankness ? When will she
Admit the nullity of that pounding sea ?

Remains of Stoppia

1 Households

Blue smokes should be rising in the gloom
Of the lower chamber, seeping between
The beams and joists of the ceiling
To cure the chestnut harvest
Spread on the floorboards of the upper room.

In its square stone shelter
The water of the well stands still,
Cool and defended from the noon-time swelter.

The people and their animals have gone,
Bound for Milan or Glasgow. Only one
Brown herd still pasture on the mountain,
Browses a high green dale,
Drinks from a circular pond.

Down in the house I found
A huge corpse festering like a smothered fire.
Shouldering and staggering through the giant heathers
And pliant whips of the broom,
A dying bullock had headed for its fall,
Hell-bent on reaching the familiar byre
And dying in its own stoney room.
The mortal hulk of it swelled from wall to wall.

2 What is Left

Three bones on the earthen floor
Tibia   scapula   vertebra
Stocky shin-bone
Eased of its meaty burden

Angular shoulder-blade
Its naked flange
As beautiful as any glass
In a cathedral window

Section of spine
With spreading tines
And tunnel for the cord

They are not lying
Like the components of a bear
Arranged in an ancient rite
They are not trying
To foretell the future
By the lie of the stones
They are purely innocent
They have their done their dying

The Heart of a Heartless Situation

1 Roman Catholics - Ukraine and Galicia

In Kiev on the Mikhailovka hill
Under an onion dome as green as cheese
A priest-shaped silhouette
Makes a black cavern in a wall of gold.
The seven worshippers huddled on their knees
Are female, scarved and old.

At Santiago in Galicia
The doorstep of the saint
Is kissed by a myriad devotees
Almost into impalpability.
Incessant leather footsoles wore their track
Across the Pyrenees and back.

From belfries on the crowds of hills
The iron mouths swing upward, gulping air,
Are swallowed backwards into throats of stone.
The beggar at the corner of the square
Rattles the small change in her yoghurt cup.
What does she hope to see when he looks up

Beyond the cardinal's marble robe,
Between the scabbard and the thigh
Of the 17th-century liberator
Bearded like God and with his petulant frown ?
Only the same faint glimmer in the sky ?
Only the turning of the same old globe ?
She counts her takings when the sun goes down.

2 Presbyterians - Scotland

It is so high in the white ceiling-hollow,
So dark up there at the root of the granite spire,
We cannot see the echoes of the psalms
And paraphrases caught like husks of flies
Sucked and discarded by the preying spiders.

Between the pinewood pillars, from the dusk
Of dark-blue velvet curtains, a sober angel
Comes out with black wings folded. His naked head
Is a dome of off-white candle-wax. His mouth
Gargles with words like 'Bans' and 'Intimations'.

The organ pumps its metallic wind and shakes
The colourless diamonds of the window-glass.
The ladies caped in fur, the gentlemen
In suits of sombre broadcloth mix their chords,
Sleep-walking pilgrims leaning on their staves.

The text is from Leviticus, the words
Unreal as schoolday Latin. In our pew
I pick my team for England v Australia
And bowl my spinners from the pavilion end
To finish, like Verity, with 8 for 40.

3 Buddhists - Sri Lanka

The idol's smile spreads and spreads, condensing
The glisten of its patina
On the mustard and ox-blood of the painted walls.
It is dew on the white lips of the temple-flowers.
Below the smile the robes - their swags of custard
Droop and congeal in layers,
Lapsing beneath the fog of the perfume.
Below the robes the limbs fold onto themselves
In stacks of uncooked pasta.

Below the smile of the yellow Buddha
Woman crouch and pray, rise up and rush
To the next shrine and the next
With a sough of yearning, a gasp of adoration,
A swallowed wail, a frenzied mutter
Of words automatic as heartbeats,
Unanimous as starlings.
Their tanned skins teem with sweat,
Their sarees swish on the sticky floor,
The lines on their foreheads strain like wires.

The priest's shaved head is a swollen fruit
Poised on the saffron stem of his robe.
He orchestrates these ardours -
Halts, and the women shrink, abased -
Moves on, and they are a cornfield in the wind -
Halts, and they are a flock beset by a dog.
They are beside themselves, their lives are chaff
On the wind of their desperate sighing
Which polishes the countenance of the Buddha,
Pleasures his lips and melts his limbs
Into a deeper and deeper trance
Of imperturbable indifference.

Time, Space and All That Stuff

Nothing is there. we balance in it
Like fish buoyed up by miles of water.
We cannot touch the hours and minutes
Or hear the sound of before and after.

It is nobody's fault. No-one began it,
Wound up the clock or signed a paper.
There was no plan for the global caper,
No bastard decided to drop us in it.

No candle-flame or prayer-wheel's spinning,
Muezzin's chant or bardic keening,
No zealot's sums or druggy dreaming
Can make an end or start a beginning.

We cannot fix it, we may not make it.
The sequence set before we began, it
Comes with terms we cannot break, it
Would be like this whatever the planet.

The ocean is dark, and what comes after
Drowning is darker. Stars are glowing.
Slowly the knowable yields to our knowing,
Slowly the fish get used to the water.

Robin's Escape

So Robin rose in his sick-bed
And levelled his bow at the open window.
Outside in the water-meadow
The willow-whips were gold
With the rising of the sap,
The primrose stars were alight
In the shadow of the hazel copses.
He would not see the dandelions
In their toothed and rampant sprouting,
He would not see the linens
Stitched to the tapestry of the hawthorns.

The black cowl of the abbess loomed in the doorway
Like a hollow tree. She was amused
That he should try to bend the bow
With the white arm her hand had bled.
She had let his life with her lancet.

The yew-wood curved, he set the nock of the arrow,
The string was taut as a pair of struts.
The steel tip and the grey goose-feather flew
Straight as a sunray. It was unravelling him,
His guts uncoiled, his sinews unbent like springs,
The curls of his hair straightened,
All of his brightness trailed from the fleeting arrow.

The abbess raged to see the arrow's landing,
Her pale eyes dazzled, stunned by sunburst.
Only his gown was lying on the mattress
Thin as a crumpled leaf.
The wand of the arrow planted in the leaf-mould,
It rooted like a sapling,
A tree among trees, at one with the forest,
While the black church cankered,
Casting its shadows, dropping its Dead-Sea-fruit.

Superpowers

Footsbarn Theatre, St Ives

So Lancelot comes prancing into the tent,
Camp as you like, eyelids a-flutter,
Blowing raspberries through his trumpet.

Guinevere was in a mood, she only
Gave her drum the occasional thump, as resonant
As a fat man falling onto an airbed.

Mordred was dressed for the occasion, his armour
Black as a fireback. His cuirasse was black
Offset by his greaves and gauntlets, which were black.

Guinevere condescended to a drumroll
Thunderous as a salvo of farts escaping
Into the thick of a feather mattress.

Mordred heaved his broadsword into the ring,
Lifted it an inch - tried harder -
Raised it another inch, and Lancelot

Whipped out his poniard, flounced at Mordred,
Stabbed at him - the rubber knife bent double -
He pouted and stamped his elegant foot.

The air was darkening, the canvas walls
Were flushed with sunset. A raven seemed to have moulted,
Choking the vault with swarthy plumage.

The heroes clanked and stumbled, their weapons dragged them
Forward and backward, their armour held them
Upright as riddled elms, as monuments

Of time-expired termites. No more faces
Scowled behind the visors. Still they brandished,
Heaving and missing, circling and stomping.

Smoke without fire filled up the arena,
Muffling the clunks and grunts. The deafened, blinded,
Dumbfounded duo must have been there - we could not

See their encumbered torsos. We could smell them
Like the breath of bronchial crocodiles,
Like flesh necrosing under a bandage.

Night in the tent. Invisible audience
Too cramped to move. The brain-dead ogres lunging.
The last we heard of them they were still at it.

Blue Morning

Jet-planes rule the sky
With white lines taut as longitude.
That cirrocumulus shoal is high -
The planes are higher, stringing
Their vapour trails like power-boat wakes
Stretched between milky atolls.
Relaxing after their battles
The gung-ho crew are singing
Smoke Gets in Your Eyes.

Body Count

The first shells flushed them out.
One of them writhed on the ground,
Struggled to his feet.
The next round from our 30mm cannon
Tore him apart.

On the hard shoulder
Bodies of creatures smaller than ourselves
Shatter silently sideways.
Abdomen and thorax
Tumble their tiny fragments
On the eddying slipstreams.
The head of a bee
Twirls in slow motion, weightlessly.

We're out there to kill their tanks and trucks.
Then we're gonna beat their goddam brains out.

The fingernail of a mole
Bounces against the diesel-blackened kerb.
The filament of a cabbage-white's antenna
Spirals into the dusty grass.

Into the Shredder

He had reached that beautiful time of day
At last when everything settled down, gave up.
People too fagged to argue any more
Sat back and eyed their computer screens,
Letting the servers swim past silently.
The phones had quietened to the occasional trill.

Shredder time. He had emptied all the bins
Of obsolete memoranda, agendas, drafts,
Yesterdays' papers, personal letters even -
He never looked at those (except the signatures),
He was the soul of confidentiality.

The bunched shreds teemed and streamed
Like tagliatelle from a pasta-maker.
Suddenly they were boiling scarlet.
Hot juice spurted and spewed
From every joint and louvre,
Vomited from the vent, drooled down the flex.
He clapped his hands on the holes.
Jets of it sprang between his fingers,
Red rain blinded his glasses.
It reached his mouth, he licked it -
Salty and tangy, living gravy - he retched.

He looked round - nobody watching.
Still the machine poured, seething.
What had he put in last ? The colour supplements.
Were the pictures from Bosnia or Rwanda ?
Ethiopia ? Kurdistan ? East Timor ?
Serbia ? Sudan ? Colombia ? Burma ?
Iraq ? Uganda ? Chechnya ?

Impossible to remember. Only the faces
Stared back at him - black convicts
Hauling corpses out of the ground.
A dozen children with squints and harelips
In an empty room with filthy walls.
A toothless monk with his cheeks caved in...
They had all gone into the pulp.
They were in there somewhere, unrecognisable.
And he himself was a hopeless mess -
How could he face his colleagues ? How on earth
Could he go out into the street like this ?

The Greek Comrades

Lancaster, 1971

Pavlos works with his fiddle,
Mikis with his guitar.
The bow is a daring rapier
Innocent of all blood.
The fingers jump and alight,
An independent animal.

Mikis and Pavlos look at each other,
Mouths half-smiling,
Black eyes glistening,
Seeing a hot white street
Seventeen hundred miles south-east
Barred by the shadows of policemen.

Pavlos and Mikis let the notes
Shower from them, incessant treads
Of a staircase mounting against them, with them,
Speeding the crowd of us upwards -
The belt of it streams in a blur -
We shake and adjust to its giddy momentum.

Mikis and Pavlos watch us, lead us
Round in the loop, we are upside-
Down, we are headlong, inventing
Steps for the freedom reel.
Their ears are leaning, hearing
Sandbags hit the head of a prisoner.

Footsoles slur on the carpet,
We lick the sweat from our eyebrows
And come to rest in a daze of stillness.
Pavlos and Mikis smile and remember
The boots and shades and tunics
Black on black in the radiant city.

Times and Creatures

Tired workers on the building sites
Divide their lives in hours
While carpenter and bumble bees
Drain the rosemary flowers.

Each summit of the marble sgurrs
Is cleft in blocks of white
And drills and diamond saw outscream
The eagle and the kite.

Blue blades of sunlight rake the woods,
The chainsaws bite and snore.
We share the pastures and the glades
With porcupine and boar.

We greet the wild duck and the seals
With scatter-guns and knives,
Feeding our inexhaustible guts
With other creatures' lives.

Who will outlast humanity
To populate the dark
And shapeless space of future time ?
The cockroach and the shark.

Who will move in to colonise
The stone-and-timber house
We shared with dogs and singing-birds ?
The kestrel and the mouse

While terraced olive-branches chant,
Each glinting leaf a note
In an unconscious aria
Sung from a finch's throat.

The Height of the Great Moss

The scalp of hoar is permanent on Cairn Toul
Whether the weather on the Moine Mhor
Is blowing fine or foul.
The blade of the glacier dozing over
Laid bare that stony flay.
Its skull of granite weathered old-man-grey
Before the ptarmigan flew in from Jutland,
Even before the pine.
It is the colour of a silenced brain,
Bloodless and motionless as the coffined dead.
It is the grizzled head
Of an old peasant who will not be moved
Even by civil war,
Who is bothered not at all
What politicians and banks are fighting for.
I have breathed this air before :
On Burrival midway down the western islands,
Little square belvedere above the waters
Where crofters cleared from Sollas
Wintered along Loch Eport, passed on south,
And left it to its silence ;
On Morven in the second year of war
Where we laid fenceposts up the summit slope
In Vs for Victory,
Paused to let in the stillness of the moor,
And heard a single Heinkel grunt and snore,
Black as a condor in the summer sky.
The Great Moss lours above them all,
Spreading its blanket for a giant's bed.
Here I will lay my own expiring head
Only in fantasy
When life dissolves in ideal resignation
And dreams of dying as it ought to be -
No filth, no struggle, only embarkation
Onto the inland sea.

Time to Recover

for Norman Iles

Come back, Norman, from the treacherous grooves
Where your injured mind spirals,
Where your feet shuffle
Amongst the frozen leaves of dictionaries
And your hand trembles as it feels
The starry patterns of rime melt and slur.

On the ladder of too many syllables
Rotten rungs are missing and you cannot
Get back down securely.
Those big words never helped you,
Pompous parodies of your natural tongue,
Unhinging it at its root.

Come back from the other end of the Prom
Where the wintry sunset starts to fade
The moment it excites you,
Sending you home again, luring you out again.
You should inhabit the world of leaves and branches
For 'That is fundamental.'

Those were your own words as you dwelt
On a green photo of rowan, birch and holly.
Mary will drive you to the woods in summer,
The smell of badger and deer will speak to you
As distinctly as the prints of language
And you will enter your own poems again.

Norman Dead

'... a motion and a spirit that impels
All thinking things, all objects of all thought,
And rolls through all things.' (Wordsworth)

His dead hand feels much heavier
As though the blood in there had chilled to slag.
His forehead, even stronger now,
Curves in a small vault.
Are there still eyes beneath his eyelids ?
How can an eye not see ?
That stubborn nose-arch will not flinch
At the coffin's closure.

Would it be frivolous to shake his hand ?
I only cup the back of it, no longer
Expecting a hearty squeeze.
Lungs and knees and genitals,
The same frost grips them all,
Cold beyond cold. This 'thinking thing'
Is only a thing now, seeming wholly himself,
A perfect likeness, a memorial.

Towards the End

for James Simmons

His eyes are clouded sapphires pointing south
From the gutted lighthouse of his skull.
His brain may still be brimming full
And the quirk at the corner of his mouth
Is trying to speak or kiss.
In the swimming, sailing, singing years
We did not know that it would come to this
In a Letterkenny hospital ward.
His lips are trying to open in a yawn -
Long before supper he is bored, bored, bored.

So does he rage or chafe
At the curse of his subarachnoid haemorrhage ?
For many months to come
He will be sitting in this chair at home
Immersed in love and tedium,
Struggling to concentrate and read aloud
Page 11 of *Far from the Madding Crowd.*

Freeze-Frame

for Bill Peascod

Beneath the hundred-and-fifty-metre steep
A man moils. If he were his father,
He would be riving at it till the drift
Hollowed under the sea or coal-fall killed him.

The only levels here are blue walkways
Which the sun's hub radiates between
The summits of the ridge from Eagle Crag
To Sheepbone Buttress. If they were firm as rock
Bridging across the Combe's echoing cauldron,
I could reach the man with the miner's calves
Swollen from bracing him in the three-foot seam.

There is no adit here. The airs of space
Nourish wings on his shoulders, suck at his feet.
He soldiers upwards. Soon he will reach the light.
Soon it will leave him. 'In the pit you were nothing -
On the crag you were the master.' Beams
Of dust roof in his vertical world and slabs
Of Cumbrian slate bear down upon his shoulders.

When we have gone down with the sun, he will
Be lodging there as though he had never moved.

Together

The man at the front of the crowd was into the music,
Shoulders jigging easily to the drumbeat.
His full brown hair was faded hay, his skin
Was beige, the ghost of a tan. He might have been
A traveller who had mapped the Empty Quarter,
An expert in the fungi of East Greenland.

While his legs sat quietly in his trousers,
His trunk and hands were tapping it, rapping it,
Free as the rastas, children and women,
Bopping next to the fountain. His little girl,
Straw-blonde with a brilliant smile, was bringing her face
Close up to his, he leaning towards her, singing
Wordlessly to the rhythm. As she stood
In her leaf-green summer dress, he urged his wheelchair
Round in a circle, girl at the centre, standing
At her ease, with a little smile of collusion.

The band signed off. In the ripple of the clapping
The man and the girl moved on, her hand on the chair-arm,
Her wrist relaxed and lissome. As they passed
Beyond the Museum they were still talking.

Last Things

The ice-sheet thickening behind my eyes
Covers a buried life, a slow extinction,
Fossil pollen of family memories,
Dormant seeds of forgettings.
Lightning in November beyond the shutters…
Black water heaving past a porthole…
Pressure of heat in the middle of my forehead
As I begin to cry…
Trickle of urine running down my thigh.

Daddy is dressing up as a gentleman
In sand-brown checked plus-fours.
He goes out to the spruces with his 12-bore
Immaculately oiled and burnished shotgun.
At gloaming in the roedeer glade
He has killed a wild wood-pigeon - blaeberries
Haemorrhage from its shattered head.
One day I found a dell in the bracken
Where the deer harboured, warm and dry.
I lay in it till a heron crossed the sky.

When Mummy has tucked us up at night
She reads from *The Wind in the Willows*.
The wild wood smells of toadstools.
We are allowed to mark the evening's chapter
With an HB pencil cross. Or it is Alice
Talking to sheep behind the looking-glass.
The gas-fire burbles - chicken-pox and fever
Wax and diminish in its pointy flames.
Downstairs again, we play victorious games,
Inking red arrows on the war-maps,
Shelling and capturing Nazis, Wops and Japs.

Mother's mother, stoned in the street at Rosemount
For being German, ended up babbling it
In the old folks' home - *'Gesegnete mahlzeit,*
Bless their little tummies…'
And Uncle Graham, hit
By one of the last bullets at Craonne -
Was that his Sam Browne lolling out of the humus
Next to the hollow of a trench
Like a half-severed tongue ?

Father's mother, lying between linen,
Smoothing and smoothing at the counterpane
With her forefinger, saw again -
She and her sister as they went to school
Across the fields of Kincardine -
A hailstorm darkening and swarming,
Bouncing and hissing off the granite stones
That walled their cabbage-garden…
Their brains, their images are somewhere,
Ashes or compost, ground with the world's grains.

Lobal cooling whitens the grey
Like snow on hoarfrost,
And when I am cold as butcher-meat,
My skin as smoothed and sere
As winter petals on a hellebore,
My head as blind as a boulder,
I will not be hearing
What Anne or any of the children say
When they have kissed my brow respectfully
And turned at last away.

The Dance of the Proteins

The glistening strands unwind and wind again,
Printing the forms of the species. They print
The lark and the gooseberry saw-fly,
    the earthworm and the osprey,
    sickle-cell anaemia and the yellow Labrador ;
they print the horse and the turtle,
    the basking shark and the human...
In the spiralling formulae of the amino-acids
the elements nimble forward, upward
    in a dazzle of glissandi.
Deep in the muddy bass
ragworm and razor-fish twitch
    to the high-sea-sharp of becoming -
the black and the white notes sink and surface -
the feathered arms of the lizard
are born again in the wings of the condor -
a mote in the eye of the orca flipping a seal
    in the breakers of El Niño...
Borne on the sluice of the undercurrent,
    the blue and the green sea-juice,
the dance of the molecules mingles and joins
in the file of the enzymes, it snakes to the head of the concourse,
it splits and resumes in the whorls of the couples.
It is all there, all of it, every -
the Day of the Dead and the Summer Solstice,
    the grains of the Quern-dust Calendar and the hands
    of the marram arcing on the dials of the dunes ;
    the dog-fish cast up on the Strand of the West
    and the caul of my son's birthing.
Cirrus and maidenhair, tangle and DNA,
the plumes of us shake, shake down, shake out
    and the ends of them are beyond us.